Poems Verses Words of Rhyme
The second of a choice

Poems Verses
Words of Rhyme
Passed by the basics

Jumpin Media
Books 2018

Poems Verses Words of Rhyme

A Pocket Book of Poems
Passed by the basics

Jumpin Media
Books 2018

Acknowledgements

With thanks to everyone and anyone, we are all as important as the next person.

Special thanks to me two sisters & two brothers, Mum & Dad, step Mum & step sisters, three adult children, one ex-wife and girlfriends, family & friends, and anyone who knows me or has met me, past and present, good or bad, happy and sad, experiences learnt and still learnng.

Where ever I be, where ever I roam, you're in my heart, my heart of home. xx

Also a big thanks to KDP Amazon, in more ways than one, they help people put their written work into book form and help connect us to the outside world.

Let the poems begin

'Covers for our protection'

Living under an invisible roof
Layers of an Ozone Dome
The umbrella of life
covers for our protection

White bed linen sheets
The feathered wings of an Angel
The embracing arms of a loved one
Covers for our protection

Under colours of a Rainbows arch
White clouds of a sunlit day
Or the stars on a moonlit night
Covers for our protection

Even rings of a shining halo
The heart strings of adoration
The spoken words of wisdom
Covers for our protection

We're all living under an invisible roof
Not visible works of construction
But protected all the same
With covers for our protection

'Image of Oneself'

Image of oneself
In a looking mirror
You'll see your other ego
Standing by your side

An evening's reflection
Through mirrored glass
Depicting demons
Not just in reflection
But standing side by side
Nowhere can you hide

The person that you see
An exact copy maybe
Look into those eyes
Does the mirror tell lies?

'Scratch'

Scratch the surface, but not too deep
You never know, what monsters you'll meet
Some big and brawn, some small and weak
But you never know, what monsters may seek
Scratch the surface, but not too deep

'Reaching Goals'

Rolling down a steep road
On a bicycle with legs akimbo
Holding tight the handle bars
Shouting words of high karumba

Reaching level bottom in a whizz
As the bike slows down
A laugh on a stunned face
And a smile upon a frown

Trudging up a rocky hill
With a stick in one hand
Puffing and panting, left and right
Not the idea you had planned

Reaching top out of breath
With time to sit and rest
Recoiling like an unwound spring
To recoup that self lost zest

Getting there by going nowhere
Whether up or down a hill
As life stories do unfold
With the tales of Jack and Jill

Reaching a point of self control
To steer a new course
Up and down, in and out

At life's pleasure we endorse

'Fracking'

Protesters tents encamp
Men and women on the road
Daily traffic slow to pass
Shouting voices morally ignored

Police parked vans and cars
Alerted for any public affray
Uniformed officers stand silently
Waiting actions of the day

Business men and women
Trying to make some progress
Onto site amid protests
Against so much duress

Media reports on the protests
Mainly on the bad
One day this will be over
Which a lot of people will be glad

Fracking, a word of gas
From the depth of shale
Either for or against
It's left for Mother Nature to prevail

'Blue Dress'

Smart blue dress
Smart blue dress
Now all I gotta do
Is find a woman to impress

Slim, curves, bones 'n 'all
Gotta find a woman
Whose six foot tall

Angelic in looks
And soft swaying hair
Gotta find a woman
With style and flair

For this blue dress
Deserves the best in chic
Worn to be stunning
Any day of the week

'Caring'

When people care
It's not words that take centre stage
It's their actions

The little things a person does
Speaks volumes

Although words are comforting, reassuring
Action speak louder

We are all caring in our own way
Every day, without thought

The simplest action
The simplest smile
Well worth caring
Surely worthwhile

'Spirit Stranger'

Blown in on a swirling wind
Landing with a gentle drop
Like the grace of a white horse
Galloping on the trot

A guardian from the Angels
Showing your prescience felt
Looking out for signs of trouble
And offering all your help

The shadows of your aura
Embracing in your arms
Like being in a bubble
And wrapped in unbeatable charms

With a protected shield of love
An armour casing of hope
A belief in the power of thought
And the warmth of a winters coat

So stranger on a white horse
Fighting against the yin and yang
Delivering the good from the evil
Balancing the best you can

You keep safe a troubled soul
With feeling in the air
And watch over the beginnings

With a sense of someone's there

So spirit stranger
Riding on a white horse
I feel your supporting guidance
Through life's, sometimes, rocky course

'Birds Nest'

Grass grows on the roof top guttering
The higher a bird can nest
With not so many trees
Their choice is second best

As scaffold climbs the side building
Covered in a green mesh
Men get to work on the roof top
Now the birds have nowhere to nest

Away fly to another roof
Or desperately yonder a tree
To make a home for yourself
Where you can live and be free

No room in towns or cities
For the nesting of our birds
No home for them to go to
Just humans in their herds

So give thought to the land we live
The trees and the areas they surround
As there's lots of little creatures
Hidden, living and in abundance, abound

'Pay your way'

Gate money takings
Revenues, proceeds
Pay your way
I hear you say

Before you cross the gate
One foot in, one foot out
It's never too late

Fence or barrier
Wall or door
You pay your way
Before you go

'Move Over'

Going to the other side, of the hedge
Over to the other side, of the roses
From the colours of the reds
To the colour of the whites
Where the coffee smells better
Over the hills and far away
Where the grass is a lot greener
But that's what people just say

'Young people'

Give them guidance in life
But not your way of living
They will find their own way
Just like we all do

Be there when they need you
Comfort them when they need comforting
Agree to disagree
About each other's views

Make them feel loved
Wanted and warm
No matter what problems occur
Be strong in your decisions
Be strong in your choice of words

For at the end of the day,
Young people become parents too
And that's the future
Of all family stories
Told down the generation line

Because we are all young
We are all old
Sometime in our short life's
Enjoy all the ups and downs
Enjoy the joy of living
Enjoy the youth of young people

Then they will embrace
The age of older people

'Aches and Pains'

If pain is a killer, I would have died many times over
Headaches, backache, toothaches and much more
All have been knocking at my health door

All of a sudden as I've got old
The aches and pains, have took a big hold

Some days are fine, some days are not
But more than anything, I get the lot

What you telling me, as my body talks
It's not time to slow down on my walks

So far my strength has seen me through
Fought off the ailments, both grey and blue

But one day, my body will say that's enough
Let's call it quits, you body's not tough

Until the day when I lose the fight
I'm not yet ready, to say it's goodnight

So aches and pains, I got news for you
You may be strong, but I am strong too

'My Coffee'

The cough, the off and the fee
All in my morning cup of coffee
With the milk, the sugar and water
Whether a full cup, a half or a quarter

I'd happily drink a cup of tea
But later in the day for me
My system needs that body shock
To wake up my body clock

Like chocolate is for energy
Coffee is my morning allergy
Alerts my start to the day
Keeps the morning blues at bay

So along with some eggs and toast
Suppose I prefer coffee the most
But as in life and with age
I could always go back and renege

'Not alone'

Being alone isn't all too bad
You don't miss what you never had

Family, friends, work and respect
Year invitations you wouldn't expect

Take the day as events occur
Being alone is just another blur

Don't think too far in advance
And never miss an opportune chance

Loneliness is life moving on
Others busy, some passed, people gone

There's happiness within oneself
Such importance as in your health

It's only in your later years
You look on, as old age appears

With memories you're never alone
Some things are merely outgrown

If life is happy going your way
You're in control, enjoy your day

'Still Viable'

In the midst of life
Among the latter years
Stuck in an arm of rotation
Spinning the wheel of tears

You've passed the teens
Upset a midlife crisis
Caught up with the age
Where a problematic life is

Still full of the wonders
That life has to give
Just like to move on
And continue to live

With plenty to give
And plenty to take
You can still rock 'n'n roll
Quiver and shake

So comes no surprise
Life seems to be on hold
It doesn't have to be this way
Now that you are old

'Tell Me'

When I kiss you goodnight
You turn off the tree lights
And all the spirit just seems to go
You wave me good cheer
As I hold back a tear
Leaving my footprints in the snow

Will I see you again?
You're my candle light flame
Tell me sweet heart I need to know
As my heart beats so fast
And the time has just passed
I turn and hold out the mistletoe

We then kiss once again
I spoke out your name
All the love seemed to flow
I took hold of your hand
We had nothing planned
Our love I cannot ignore

So I'll ask you my dear
Can we marry next year?
Tell me sweet heart I need to know

'The Plan'

That's the plan, stick to it if we can
No ducking nor diving, no jerking or jiving
No straying along the way

Be committed; be insipid, and fully intrepid
Not making any mistakes

Be concise and conclusive, either invasive or intrusive
But pull out all the brakes

We're going to strive to survive, push the plan along
Stick to the route outlined

No diversion, deviation, veering from the ideology
Strive for the sake of mankind

Be forthrightly, precisely, follow the print
Do the best that we can

Not leaving nor disbelieving, for a quick exit
Because we'll always stick to a plan

'Wollen Hat'

Where's me wobbly hat
Me bobbly hat
Me cap of many colours
Me ears warmer
Me head warmer
Me cap thats multi-coloured

'Tick Tock'

I feel like a ticking alarm clock
On the inside, a facade of entirety
Everything that should be right, is right
Working together as one unity

A machine that seems to be working
All visual parts playing their role
A stern face looks astute
But the inside, is not working at all

Inner faults are slowly breaking down
An invisible health malfunction
Crossed signals causing mayhem
Fusing wires, at the box junction

A dormant volcano lays waiting to erupt
To attack, the system inside
Replacing blood with molten larva

That's the moment, your body dies

So get checked those little ailments
Before they grow out of control
It's worth taking notice
Rather than taking a fall

Don't let the clock, ring time on you slowly
You've more hours left in the day
There's years left to set an alarm
Set your clock, in reverse from today

'Your Path'

You can be who you want to be
Working towards your own goal
Slowly building up the foundations
Leading into you chosen role

Don't expect a smooth and even run
As life has her ups and downs
If you can work to overcome them
You can turn your life around

Stride with steps easy to walk in
Moving forward, at a level pace
Don't run to get there any quicker
All winners, don't always win the race

Life's about the bridges you build
Making a connection, of where to go
Reaching forward along a path
Across to places, that you know

Any route is worked hard
To achieve a life, that's so apt
So take a hand for yourself
To a life you can self adapt

'Bus Journey'

Got on a bus today
A different route
Different number
But going to the same place
As my usual bus does
Even the same bus company

Showed my ticket, took my seat
Sat second row, near the window
On the left hand side of the bus
Got as comfortable as I could
You're not paying for comfort
But you may as well, use the privilege

Although there was rain on the window
A little steamed up
It was still visible to see out
Not that there's much to see

On these bus journeys
That you haven't seen before
Houses, gardens, trees, cars
They all remain the same
Seen one, seen them all
But you look out the window, anyway
Just in case you miss something
You haven't seen before

A change of scenery
A change of bus route
Makes the journey feel different
Or is that the boredom

You're looking, you're hoping
That there is something
You haven't seen
Taking a different route
Than you normally would
To get to where you are going
From a to b, on a different bus number
A different route
Just for a change

'Coastal Waters'

Leaning against a metal rail, taking in the sights
In the distant bay, I see mountainous heights

Pampas grass blowing, as the sea makes its ebb
Looking like the coils, on a spiders silky web

Sea birds soaring, atop the warm air flow
Looking down, as if to say hello

Sand dunes drift on a walker's path
Like the angry devil, showing his wrath

Lone figures walking, one leading their dog
Some looking a little amused, others looking agog

The only stillness you will see
Are the stones, not moving so free?

A flag once flying wraps around its pole
And water, has filled that little pot hole

A quick whiff of early morning toast
Just some of the activity
You'll see around Britain's coast

'Deliberately'

Deliberately
I sat on the chair
Deliberately
I put my feet upon the table
Rocking my chair, back and forth
Deliberately
I didn't mean to fall off
And hurt my arm

'The Sun'

The Suns ray for a moment
Bursts through my window pane
Highlighting the furnishings
Then suddenly, disappeared
Was there a lapse in the bad weather?
The Sun finding its way
Through the grey clouds
Sitting, waiting for the moment
To shine once more

'In your dreams'

Thank Heaven for dreams
Where you can escape to
Get away from the pains in life

Chill out for a while from everything
Be who you want to be
Only have the things
You want in a dream

But in reality
As dreams don't come true
Not that often anyway

You are not escaping
Your real life
You are not changing
Your real life

You are merely
Having a moment
A rest from being
Like everyone else

Looking for something better
Where your life is different
From the one you live

Be it a happy dream

Be it a sad dream
It's escapism from the now life
Which we all need
Every now and then

'Lost in chat'

Temporary lost in chat
Happily chatting away
Focused on what's being said
And what people say

But there's a talking queue
A traffic jam
Like water being held
By a walled concrete dam

Trying to cut in
With my words not being heard
Pushed to the back
By stampeding internet herds

Not noticing any others
Nor the life in my surround
Because internet chatting
Is everywhere and abound

Eventually my line gets back
To my usual self norm
I'm lost in chat
That I lovingly adorn

'Out and about'

Out and about mix and mingle
Meeting people, who like to jingle
Having some time for a social spell
Helping to achieve, some goals as well

Out and about ducking and diving
With certain people, twisting and jiving
Having time for a little leisure
Enjoying the fine times, at life's pleasure

Out and about wheeling and dealing
Made some friends, with love and feeling
Using my time to say hello
Being cheerful as I go

Out and about to meet and greet
Been a long time, on my feet
I've found new friends like I said
Time to rest my weary head

Being so active out and about
Takes its toll and takes its clout
When meeting people, doing something new
Maybe one day we'll be friends too

When we're out and about
With which I have no doubt

'Getting Old'

If getting old
Is just about, aches and pains
Keeping fit and party games
I'd rather skip, those irksome years
And just sit back, with a couple of beers
Eating cakes and sipping tea
Falling asleep, in front of a TV
Rest assured in times like these
Its Cod Liver oil and Seven Seas

'Sun Energy'

The Sun rests on my face, as I lay
Taking in the warm rays
My skin absorbing the heat
The rest of my body
Wanting a share of the pleasure
The Sun is giving off

Do I strip naked?
And let the whole of my body
Absorb the Sun rays
Or do I continue to lie as I am
Letting my body
Distribute the goodness
That my face benefits

Just relax not caring
Or really thinking about anything
The heat sets a positive energy
Into my whole body

My soul stores it for my after life
While my wellbeing
In this life
Gets a needed energy boost
A recharging of the inner battery
That helps keep things, in working order
And the body works together
As one again

'Tis a Menu'

Tis a menu, a bill of fare
Not the beak of a bird
On a ride at the fair

Tis a list, a list of choice
Not the leaning of a boat
Happened to be called rejoice

Tis a menu, to feast with your eyes
Look over the creations
With glee and surprise

Tis a list, to pick and to choose
An order of the highest
An order of the foods

Thank you chef

'Wait for me'

Wait for me in heaven
And when I get there
At the end of my life
I will come and look for you

If I happen to go the other way
For some reason
I will sell my soul, seek you out
To be in your arms once again

The times we have spent together
In this life we've lived
Will be reflected and continued
In the next life we live

Our souls will come together
Destined to be re-united
In the afterlife

So wait for me my darling
As we find each other again

No one can break our freedom
The bond we have is strong
Our love will always continue
Through the short days and the long

So wait for me in heaven

'My Valentine Love'

You give me, your warm hearted feelings
You give me, your warm hearted love
Without your warmth in my life
My life is not enough

You speak, the warmest of words
You have the gentlest of touch
You are the world in which I live
That's why I love you so much

You're more, than just my valentine
And I'm glad to be with you
I cannot express my feelings
You're my love, all the year through

'Your Own'

Live by your own judgement
Your own views
And your own words
Then your life
Will be a happy one
And you are
In control of it

Live by another's judgements
Another's views
And another's words
Then they
Are the happy ones
And they are in control
Of your own life

'Appreciated'

Appreciate, the life of today
No need to change for anything

Appreciate, life's ups and downs
That keeps your feet firmly grounded

Appreciate, the chances wrongly taken
All the chances lost or mistaken

Appreciate, time left on Earth
All the values that time is worth

Appreciate, being treated with respect
With high regard, with no disrespect

Attach importance to any esteem
Try hold dear what you deem

As life's passage, through Earth's time
Is appreciated, whether your time or mine

'I don't'

Don't do hugs
Nor goodbyes
Might swear
Talk loud-tinnitus
Say it as it is
So take me as you find me
Oh, and don't
Let another's gossip
That stigmatises a person
Cloud your own
Way of thinking

'Dancing Wind'

As the wind howls outside
My top floor flat window
Howls but does not blow
I ponder could I not?
Be any closer to heaven
Than I already am

Sat listening to the winds
High and low various tones
Compelling the moans and groans
Seeing visions of a wild
Raging dancing fire
Except there is no fire

Forming a figure
Moving to the sound of the wind
Is she window knocking
Beckoning me to join her
For a last final whirl
A farewell twirl

Shall I dance the dance?
Of the storms with her
Like a tempest affair
Visual only in my mind
Image of a howling gale
But alas prevail

Her dancing has a slow tone
A slow dance
A goodbye romance
Then suddenly blowing out
As if to talk lightly
Whispers so quietly

No longer the howling wind outside
My top floor flat window
Just blowing, slowly blowing
Down to a gentle breeze
A silent lull
Tis the final annul

'If ever there be'

There once was an unmarried woman
A Spinster if ever there be
Now in her formative years
But still attractive to see

She's loved, she's lost, and she's languished
Never the right man came along
To hold her heart so dearly
Nor sing in tune to her song

One day she met an unmarried man
A Bachelor if ever there be
A little younger than herself
But none the less, the missing key

Both had a magnet of attraction
Each connecting with one another
With politeness and understanding
A romance of a first time lover

The numbers began to make sense
All of two being equal to both
They decided to get together
And made their union under an oath

Her heart now set for racing
Beating that extra beat
Through the love of a Bachelor man

That she had come to meet

Now still a Spinster of age
Her life will glow once again
With rosiness in her cheeks
And a love ready to be lain

'Just Mountains'

As the mountains
Either side of the pass
Scallop, to meet the road
At the bottom
Leaving scars
As they reach a point
To where the road levels

Remains of snow visible
Still filling the deep scars
Waiting to melt
To join the stream
On its voyage
From mountain to river to sea

Mountains are more visible
If only you would look
Closer as mountains stand out
With such an attraction
Such fullness
Solidarity in their stance

Forever being mighty
Through all the seasons
Just mere mountains
A beauty for all to see

'Life comes good'

Going about daily life
Living the hours of today
Not thinking far ahead
Nor concerned of any affray

Politeness is in your manner
Respect to people you talk
Ignorance is not of nature
Or n your line of thought

Regardless of the voices
From people that don't know
Limited in their absence
Of the factual picture show

An aura of some belief
Surrounds you like a shield
Turns around the dismissive
And spreads them far afield

A triumphant bugle blows
The power force of a soul
Its entirety is of one
And completion is a whole

'Oh a word of Love'

Love, is just another four letter word
Could be classed as a swear word,
To some people
Some people only use it
When they have done something
And their partner finds out
I love you
As they try to wriggle out
Of an awkward situation
Trying to change the stories view
And deception so they don't get found out
Using the word love in a conversation
Not within the proper context
Other than when it's meant to be used
Is to put off guard
A partner who has been lied to

Love, is also a beautiful four letter word
To be used
When it truly does mean what it says
Especially to your partner in life
No other four letter word
Could mean so much
To another person in a romance
It's a form of showing by words
How much a person means to you
Embracing them wholly
In awe of their ever being

Everything about them
You whole heartedly are in love with
Their sheer existence in your life
They are part of you
Without them, there would be no love

'Speculation'

Is it a reason to speculate?
On things we don't know
Or guesstimate
Without watching the show

We can of course assume
Just as we can guess
Upon thoughts taken for granted
To set right the redress

But as humans, I doubt
We care to surmise
That telling of others
Through imaginative eyes

Collectable showings
Without knowledge of others
We fair to impress
The acts of another
But speculate the same

'Tattoo or Taboo'

Tattoo or taboo
It's just about the art, for me

Paintings on walls
Pictures in frames
It's all classed as art
Just the same

Contemporary to modern
A language in paint
Even church windows
Depicting a saint

So tattoo or taboo
Art forms all around
Even in our voices
Most art can be found

'Fleetwood Pier'

Once stood a slightly figure
Of iron, paint and rust
Encroaching, hunkering
All tide and time, wasn't it just

Adorned like a budding flower
As years had gone by
Shadowing, for all to see
In a moonlit sky

Rose up from the sand
Upsurge in the sea
Stood elevated and proud
Honouring by degree

Embraced the four seasons
Of any given year
What a delight for those
Who loved Fleetwood Pier?

'Time to sit and reflect'

Sat on a wooden curved bench
My back resting on the concrete, curved wall
On the other side
The sound of a mower, being pushed along
The grass edged kerb
By a man in a yellow safety jacket

The smell of freshly cut grass
Competing against the sea salt
On an incoming tide
Waves rush to shore
As if late for an appointment
Dressed in a mix of drab blues, grey and green

One solitary green and white boat
Slowly sailing, passed towers of wind turbines
On the distant horizon

Looking up to a bright sky
Mixed in the colours of blues, greys and white
I take a sip from my fizzy orange
To take away the taste of sea salt
Blowing in the gentle breeze

I then stand up
To get a little movement back in to my legs
Before I walk away
Passing the waste bin

I put in my empty plastic orange bottle

I once sat on a curved wooden bench

'Nowhere'

Caught up in a hypnotic world
Trance like wanderings
Going nowhere except back
To where you once started from

'Knowledge'

Knowledge, is good in the early life
Then in the latter life
Knowledge doesn't get used much
Yet it still has its place in our brain
Sitting on a back ledge
Just waiting to be used once again

'I had a glimpse'

I had a glimpse, took a look
Glanced at the unforeseen
Through the darkness of the day
And the surprise of a dream

Although the sight turned out cold
You can never really tell
When light resembles darkness
Some thoughts I'd rather not dwell

Even though my glimpse was short
It still gave me an insight
To whether doing good or bad
We all have demons to fight

Life cannot be together perfect
It just doesn't work that way
Both good and bad are needed
Like shades of white, black and grey

Luckily my glimpse was not so full
Showing any life I may have
Because living with life's mysteries
Is one of the reasons to be glad?

'Seaside Bench'

I sit here, stretched out
On this sea side bench
A person walks by
With a dog on a lead
A Poodle
'Are you comfortable sir?'
They said
'Yes indeed I am'
I reply
Onwards they walk
A spring in their step
Maybe I amused them
In some way
Glad to be of service
And enlighten someone's day

'A Laugh'

Sometimes
Jokes are not funny
And I ponder
Whether to laugh
For the sake of laughing
Do I just gather a sigh?
And shrug my shoulders
No, I laugh after a pause
Then I sigh and wonder why
I didn't just say
I don't get it

'A closed door'

I came across a closed door
Am I stood on the outside, or the inside?
Without opening it, I wouldn't know
I stand and look at the closed door
I leave it closed and walk away
It will still be there tomorrow

'Deepest deep' Loch Ness

Within a land of mystery
And depths so deep
Mountains strike out
Towering over the land

Can the secrets of the loch
Stay hidden, stay secret

Legends, folklore and tales are abound
The mysteries that surround
This beautiful, mysterious land

There's a water horse, galloping
Beneath the loch shores
Racing in the depths
That no one person goes

It's within the waters magic
From those awe inspiring tales
Spoken about a creature of old
From where this monster hales

In this such loch
Most beautiful with suspense
Could live a creature
That's mystically intense

That's part of the beauty

And part of people's lives
Within the grasps of those
That believes, in the legend of the past

So water horse, keep safe
The magic and the myth
Remain dear in the hearts
Of generations and their kith

'Talk for the sake of talking'

Your mouth racing
Down the alphabet, highway
More words pacing a rate
Your feet would not catch up
Why would you talk?
For the sake of talking
Except, to hear one's own voice
Music to your own ears
But not to everyone's
What words are spoken, is irrelevant
Like a chatterbox fully wound up
A spring that continually
Recoils, back and forth
Without pause
For thought or breath
Talk for the sake of talking
Is hard work and can be
For the untrained voice box

'Birthday'

Another year old tomorrow
And I'm walking on a beach
While the view to the Lakes
And Trough, is great and inviting
I reflect on what I'm doing here
And still, I don't have the answer
My instincts, my senses
Tell me I don't belong here anymore
People walk past, with a purpose to their life
I walk with the aim
To find a purpose, to my life

'Stick with it'

Whatever's thrown at us in life?
No matter who throws it?
We are programmed, to just carry on

Whether debt, death or illness
We just carry on
We are not programmed
In our brains
To sit back and do nothing

We just persevere like before
Continue the best we can
Stand up, be the man
Or woman

Best to stick with it
Until life is at a style
We feel right with
Withstand a false smile

Keep your persistence
Keep your growling bear
That hungers your stomach
And carry the day, elsewhere

'That's Life'

I'll never understand
The meaning of life
I don't think I ever will
Some day's life just bowls you over
And the next, you're in for the kill
A turn around happens before your eyes
But you don't always see it
Then almost unawares
You get a sudden sense and feel it
Suppose that's life

'I remember'

I remember the days
When the stars shone bright
Your eyes sparkled
And caught my heart
A pounding beat
That quivered my body
From my head to my toes
That was the moment
I felt your love
Something special
A warmth hit me
Like a blast of cold air
That's when I remember the days
When the stars shone bright

'Traveller'

I feel like a holy traveller
A pilgrim on a crusade
Not about to preach upon
The populace people's parade

Never the less a nomad
On the road to Mandalay
No words to recite my voyage
No words for when I pray

Travelling by the way side
Travelling a lonely gravel road
With only myself for company
And the aura of our Lord

Great strength within my strides
Great strength to see me through
As I walk the journeys end
Across a wood vale of yew

Words lead to a path of faith
Along a route of some belief
I can only see one tunnel
A tunnel that lies beneath

As a traveller
There is no real direction
Life's just one long path

In which every turn, is a connection

'Who Knows'

Without life experiences
Having lived the past
We cannot acknowledge
What we already know
And with a tweak here and there
Put those past experiences
Into words

'Big Waves'

Big waves, are rolling in
On an oceans tide
Thrusting along
Stampeding horses
With rage in their eyes

Big waves roar out loud
As they make their ebb
Then calmly before your eyes
Fade to disappearance
As they meet the shores edge

Our Statement

We treat everyone fairly, irrespective of their age,
gender or creed. We respect others; we respect where
we work and where we live. You cannot please
everyone and we wouldn't even try to do, as it's not in
our nature to make someone like us. That is who we are,
nothing more, nothing less, that is us.

Jumpin Media Books 2018 All Rights Reserved

Jumpin Media
Books 2018

Printed in Great Britain
by Amazon